ALSO BY JOHN BERRYMAN

POETRY

Poems (1942)

The Dispossessed (1948)

Homage to Mistress Bradstreet (1956)

His Thought Made Pockets & The Plane Buckt (1958)

Berryman's Sonnets (1967)

Short Poems (1967)

Homage to Mistress Bradstreet and Other Poems (1968)

His Toy, His Dream, His Rest (1968)

The Dream Songs (1969)

Love & Fame (1970)

Delusions, Etc. (1972)

Henry's Fate & Other Poems, 1967–1972 (1977)

Collected Poems 1937–1971 (1989)

The Heart Is Strange (2014)

PROSE

Stephen Crane: A Critical Biography (1950)

The Arts of Reading (with Ralph Ross and Allen Tate) (1960)

Recovery (1973)

The Freedom of the Poet (1976)

Berryman's Shakespeare (1999)

BERRYMAN'S SONNETS

JOHN BERRYMAN

Berryman's Sonnets

Farrar, Straus and Giroux

New York

Farrar, Straus and Giroux
18 West 18th Street, New York 10011

Published in 1967 by Farrar, Straus and Giroux
This paperback edition, 2014

Library of Congress Control Number: 67015007
Paperback ISBN: 978-0-374-53454-7

Farrar, Straus and Giroux books may be purchased for educational,
business, or promotional use. For information on bulk purchases, please
contact the Macmillan Corporate and Premium Sales Department at
1-800-221-7945, extension 5442, or write to specialmarkets@macmillan.com.

www.fsgbooks.com
www.twitter.com/fsgbooks • www.facebook.com/fsgbooks

1   3   5   7   9   10   8   6   4   2

To Robert Giroux

INTRODUCTION
by April Bernard

Why sonnets? Why on earth, in the middle of the twentieth century, a sonnet sequence?

In the case of John Berryman, the turning to sonnets, and more specifically, *love* sonnets, is completely of a piece with the nature of the personal crisis that prompted them. He was in his thirties; he had been contentedly married for several years; he was happily—and for him, luckily—teaching literature at Princeton. And then, out of the blue, inconveniently—and almost from the first, evidently *un*luckily—he fell in love with a young woman who was the wife of a colleague.

To a writer as self-scrutinizing as Berryman, this was a wonderful, terrifying, and guilty predicament. It was also a familiar one, at least literarily. The history of lyric poetry is, among other things, a history of passionate folly; and the best chronicles of this folly are to be found in sonnets. From the original fourteenth-century *Canzoniere* of Petrarch, to Petrarch's Elizabethan translators and emulators, to nineteenth-century writers as diverse as Elizabeth Barrett Browning and George Meredith, poets have told their tales of joy and pain, longing and doubt, praise and blame, in the story form of multiple sonnets. Functioning as a stanza in the long poem that is the sequence, each sonnet in itself, a powerfully knit, compact fourteen lines, is also designed to stand alone. Over the course of many such sonnets, a story about love unfolds along with a story about poetry as the sonnets converse with one another by repeating tropes, repeating rhymes, returning to themes with variations.

When Berryman embarked on these sonnets, he was already in the midst of his affair. Many of the early poems are explicitly addressed to the beloved, to "Lise," as he would later rename her for public eyes. In these first private envoys he writes to dazzle, to praise, and to persuade.

> This morning groping your hand moaning your name
> I heard distinctly drip . . somewhere . . and see
> Coiled in our joys flicker a tongue again,
> The fall of your hair a cascade of white flame. (#3)

> Great citadels whereon the gold sun falls
> Miss you O Lise sequestered to the West
> Which wears you Mayday lily at its breast [. . .] (#9)

But to be writing sonnets, and discovering that he was writing more than just a few, must also have disquieted the poet. It is a given of the love sonnet sequence that it *ends*, and not happily—if not in the death of the beloved, in any case in severed or unsatisfied love. Petrarch's "Laura" dies; Sidney's "Stella" rejects him; Shakespeare's two loves, the "fair young man" and the "dark lady," betray and disappoint; and even Browning's *Sonnets from the Portuguese* ends pro forma with the dismissal of the lover as the speaker embraces death—although, as everyone knows, in "real life" the poet found her happier ending. (The only prominent exception to this rule is Spenser's *Amoretti*, which culminates in marriage.) We can feel Berryman's tense relationship with his own enterprise in some of the later poems here:

How can we know with whom we ride, or soon
Or later, ever? You . . what are yóu like?
A topic's occupied me months, month's mind. (#91)

Berryman seems willfully to be prolonging the production of
these sonnets, as if the next one—like the next rendezvous with
the beloved—might turn the tide of the narrative.

In 1967, some twenty years after these poems were first writ-
ten, Berryman gathered them together, ordered them, and wrote
a few additional poems to fill out the sequence. He called them
*Berryman's Sonnets.** The title offers the winking suggestion that
"Berryman" is a character, both the poet and not the poet (as
Henry in the *Dream Songs* is, and is not, Berryman). By naming
himself as a character, Berryman also offers in his title the first
linkage of his sequence with the one he most closely models it
on—Sidney's *Astrophil and Stella.*

Berryman's verse is filled with allusions to his literary ances-
tors—directly and indirectly, in his sonnets he also invokes Pe-
trarch, Wyatt, Shakespeare, Donne, Marvell, Sophocles, Villon,
the Psalmists, and many others, including Eliot and Pound. But
it is with Sidney—and through Sidney to their common ances-
tor, Petrarch—that he is most closely and consciously allied. The
"plot" of *Berryman's Sonnets* follows that of Sidney's sequence: pas-
sion sought; passion requited; passion delayed; and, finally, pas-

---

*It is that 1967 edition of *Berryman's Sonnets* we reprint here. A version called "Son-
nets to Chris," edited by Charles Thornbury and included in *John Berryman: Collected
Poems, 1937–1971*, combined the 1940s manuscript versions (footnoting Berryman's
own subsequent edits of these) with the later poems.

sion utterly thwarted. Borrowing one of Petrarch's many tropes, that the beloved is a shining star, Sidney casts himself as "Astrophil," the "star-lover" of "Stella," his beloved "star"; in his turn, "Berryman" loves "Lise," who also often appears to be blondly shining. In the joyful poems, she is the "unlikely sun," (#57), a "Mayday lily," on the sky's breast (#9); her face is "sun-incomparable" (#77). "You shining—where?—rays my wide room with gold" (#2). She is also a star of the night: "Astronomies and slangs to find you, dear, / Star, art-breath, crowner, conscience!" (#66). In a late poem, he longs for "[t]he pallor of your face lost like a star" (#90). In Sonnet 14, the poet figures himself as a moth fluttering about "the porchlight" that is the beloved, in a similar, more homely, but still starry guise.

Sidney permits himself to tell the reader about the difficulties he experiences in writing his poems; Berryman does this as well. Sidney's opening sonnet recounts his hopes that by writing he can change his beloved's mind, "I sought fit words . . . [b]ut words came halting forth," he complains. That sonnet ends with the ringing line: " 'Fool,' said my muse to me, 'Look in thy heart and write!' " Later he claims, in a subdued and wistful line, "Love did hold my hand and make me write."

Berryman, in Sonnet 23, struggles with the too obvious, too well-worn word "love" before his final capitulation:

They may suppose, because I would not cloy your ear—
If ever these songs by other ears are heard—
With 'love' and 'love,' I loved you not, but blurred
Lust with strange images [. . .]

Also I fox 'heart', striking a modern breast
Hollow as a drum, and 'beauty' I taboo;
I want a verse fresh as a bubble breaks,
As little false . . . Blood of my sweet unrest
Runs all the same—I am in love with you—
Trapped in my rib-cage something throes and aches!

Later, he writes, "I prod our English: cough me up a word, / Slip me an epithet" when he is searching for words to describe the beloved. In the resulting epithet, she appears, again starlike, as "cadmium shine" (#66).

Like Sidney, who upon his dismissal from his beloved's favor prowls, "exiled," beneath her window at night, Berryman in Sonnet 10, and again in Sonnet 98, alludes to climbing a sycamore tree outside Lise's house so he can look in at her. There are also numerous places in these poems where the poet has walked or bicycled somewhere for a tryst, only to be disappointed; in another, he jealously recalls hearing Lise sing one of her children to sleep. This sense of helpless exile from the life and home of the beloved colors these poems with some of their darkest, saddest shadows; Berryman here is as much an exiled son, a lost boy, as he is a lover. Indeed, he knows this, comparing his agony to that of Oedipus: ". . . only *ioú ioú* / Wells from his dreadful mouth, the love he led . . ." (#96).

Double consciousness—the knowing ambiguity of claiming that one's passion is uniquely wonderful, uniquely painful, while at the same time acknowledging that love is also, always, the same old thing—drives both Sidney and Berryman. To some extent, this ambiguity is built into the structure of the sonnet itself, here in the meditative, circular shape of the so-called Italian form. After the *volta*, or turn, that marks the break between octave and sestet, the poem modulates into an alternative attitude, which tends then to circle back around to an inconclusive conclusion, or stalemate, between the two parts of the poem. (The English, or Shakespearean, sonnet is structured more dialectically; it argues its way to a concluding couplet designed to resolve or synthesize the ambiguity set in motion by the *volta*.) It is not surprising, in Petrarch or Sidney or Berryman, for a sonnet to say, in the octave: "My suffering is unique to me, unique to our love." Then, in the sestet: "On the other hand, love has been ever thus. How about that."

The comic possibilities of the double consciousness are not unrelated, in Berryman's case, to his additional twentieth-century burden of psychoanalytic self-interpretation. Obsession, of the kind that is revealed and perhaps even fostered by the writing of these sonnets, can seem more than merely neurotic; it can seem completely mad. So if Berryman's characteristic tonal mixture of bravado and lacerating shamefacedness seems especially high-pitched in these poems, we can guess that it might be because he anticipates the judgment of the beloved and the judgment of his readers to agree with his own: that the poet is a genius, certainly, but also a nut case.

·

My own first, delighted encounter with Berryman's work was through his 77 *Dream Songs*, which I carried around with me like a private hymnal when I was in college. At Harvard's Woodberry

Poetry Room, where I spent an inordinate amount of time, the curator, Stratis Haviaras—this was in the 1970s—showed me two shoe boxes full of uncatalogued tapes of Berryman reading his poems aloud. I don't remember the sources of the tapes. But I do remember offering to help sort them, and then spending many hours for many days at a tape machine, taking notes to figure out which poems he was reading, even noting where the spoken poems varied slightly from the ones in the books—77 *Dream Songs, Homage to Mistress Bradstreet,* and *Berryman's Sonnets*—I had open on the table before me. As anyone who has listened to Berryman knows, his voice is odd and seductive. The emphasis often falls peculiarly, on the "wrong" syllable. Sometimes he mumbles, sometimes he roars, and very often he pauses mysteriously. He chuckles at his own jokes and adopts "funny" vaudeville-style voices, hamming it up like all get-out. When his voice does not sound drunken—and even when it does—it carries a keening, musical quality that seems as if it should be accompanied by percussive strums on an Irish harp.

It was not difficult for me, at the age of twenty, to adore Berryman. Succeeding years, and the acquaintance of enough writers possessing that same lethal combination of arrogance and self-abasement, have made me less susceptible. Drunkenness, also, has lost its appeal. So the persona, *as* persona—and I hasten to add that I never knew the poet, and so am not speaking of the person, but only the public poet's persona—is no longer present to charm me when I read the poems. Instead, newly, and as if for the first time, I am astonished and amazed by the poems themselves.

In reading the sonnets again, I find I can accept the persona—

"Berryman" or Berryman, whichever—as flawed. Even in those sonnets where he coldly describes the pain he inflicts on others; or self-pityingly complains about his health; or boasts, while trying to seem nonchalant, that he owes Pound three letters. And the reason I can accept the flaws is because the poetry that conveys *all* this information, about suffering, and bragging, and adoring, and despising, and whining, and lusting, and howling at the moon, is so extraordinary that it seems to make an entirely new world of thought and feeling.

Of course everything new, in poetry, is grounded in the old. "Crumpling a syntax at a sudden need" (#47), Berryman reaches back in time, past Sidney's forms to Thomas Wyatt's syntax and meter, with its free, almost jazzy quality.

> Thanked be fortune it hath been otherwise,
> Twenty times better, but once in special,
> In thin array after a pleasant guise,
> When her loose gown from her shoulders did fall
> And she caught me in her arms long and small . . .
> *(from "They flee from me . . .")*

Wyatt's famous agonized lines of remembered bliss nearly resurrect themselves in Berryman's sonnets:

> I say *I laid siege—you enchanted me* . . [. . .]
>
> I . . Only we little wished, or you to charm
> Or I to make you shudder, you to wreck
> Or I to hum you daring on my arm. *(#97)*

In Wyatt's sonnet "Some fowls there be," he writes

> For to withstand her look I am not able
> And yet can I not hide me in no dark place,
> Remembrance so followeth me of that face . . .

Since Wyatt, only Gerard Manley Hopkins and Berryman have been able to carry off a comparable sustained dis-ordering of syntax to successful effect. Berryman is most disordered when expressing himself in extremis, as did both Wyatt and Hopkins, in transports of agony or joy. The slicing-up of syntax seems for all three poets an authentic way to convey the disarrangement of the intellect in the face of powerful feeling.

> Troubling are masks . . the faces of friends, my face
> Met unawares and your face: where I mum
> Your doubleganger writhes, wraiths are we come
> To keep a festival, none but wraiths embrace [. . .] (#31)

The additional level of self-consciousness on which Berryman operates has everything to do with the self-consciousness of his century. One signal, in these sonnets, of self-consciousness is in the oddly adolescent way he cites the drinks, and sometimes the number of drinks, consumed. Here he describes his beloved—who loved music, he says, far more than poetry—in a moment of bliss:

> [. . .] spare, Time, from what you spread
> Her story,—tilting a frozen Daiquiri,

> Blonde, barefoot, beautiful,
>   flat on the bare floor rivetted to Bach. (#37)

And:

> Listen, for poets are feigned to lie, and I
> For you a liar am a thousand times,
> Scars of these months blazon like a decree:
> I would have you—a liner pulls the sky—
> Trust when I mumble me. Than gin-&-limes
> You are cooler, darling, O come back to me. (#43)

Returning again to the idea that the Italian sonnet form offers a kind of stalemate, or suspension of thought, rather than a conclusion: We can see why this form appealed to Berryman. He had seemingly resisted the very necessity of ending at all, adding poems 107 and 112–115, which explicitly round out or conclude the sequence, only later. These final sonnets, emotionally and syntactically calm by comparison with the rest, also seal his relationship with Sidney (" 'Look in thy heart and write!' ") in the final phrase: "I sat down & wrote." This is ingenious because, like the sonnet form itself, it returns us to the beginning; we may have just read what he wrote, he tells us, but since *in the poem* he is sitting down to write, emotionally we are back where we started.

As we know, Berryman later invented his own form, the "dream song." Looser than a sonnet, and also faster, it is a stripped-down and rebuilt sonnet, a serviceable three-stanza machine that can turn as often as it likes, and which neither structure nor rhyme can force to a conclusion. Dream songs are just over when they are over; they do not "end" or "conclude." (I like to think of Berryman's dream song form as "refusing" to conclude; as opposed to the Italian sonnet's gentler "thwarted wishing" to conclude.) Refusing the end is characteristic of the poet's late work. His poems become a kind of ongoing "diary," in which the poet tries to outrun mortality, and all other endings, by the mad, brave exuberance of refusing to stop.

Note

*These Sonnets, which were written many years
ago, have nothing to do, of course, with my long
poem in progress,* The Dream Songs. *Sonnet 25
appeared in the fortieth-anniversary number of*
Poetry; *the others are unprinted.*

J. B.

Ballsbridge, Dublin
October 8th, 1966

HE MADE, A THOUSAND YEARS AGO, A-MANY SONGS
FOR AN EXCELLENT LADY, WIF WHOM HE WAS IN WUV,
SHALL NOW HE PUBLISH THEM?
HAS HE THE RIGHT, UPON THAT OLD YOUNG MAN,
TO BARE HIS NERVOUS SYSTEM
& DISPLAY ALL THE CLOUDS AGAIN AS THEY WERE ABOVE?

AS A FRIEND OF THE COURT I WOULD SAY, LET THEM DIE.
WHAT DOES ANYTHING MATTER? BURN THEM UP,
PUT THEM IN A BANK VAULT.
I THOUGHT OF THAT AND WHEN I RETURNED TO THIS COUNTRY
I TOOK THEM OUT AGAIN. THE ORIGINAL FAULT
WILL NOT BE UNDONE BY FIRE.

THE ORIGINAL FAULT WAS WHETHER WICKEDNESS
WAS SOLUBLE IN ART. HISTORY SAYS IT IS,
JACQUES MARITAIN SAYS IT IS,
BARELY. SO FREE THEM TO THE WINDS THAT PLAY,
LET BOYS & GIRLS WITH THESE OLD SONGS HAVE HOLIDAY
IF THEY FEEL LIKE IT.

BERRYMAN'S SONNETS

I wished, all the mild days of middle March
This special year, your blond good-nature might
(Lady) admit—kicking abruptly tight
With will and affection down your breast like starch—
Me to your story, in Spring, and stretch, and arch.
But who not flanks the wells of uncanny light
Sudden in bright sand towering? A bone sunned white.
Considering travellers bypass these and parch.

This came to less yes than an ice cream cone
Let stand . . though still my sense of it is brisk:
Blond silky cream, sweet cold, aches: a door shut.
Errors of order! Luck lies with the bone,
Who rushed (and rests) to meet your small mouth, risk
Your teeth irregular and passionate.

Your shining—where?—rays my wide room with gold;
Grey rooms all day, green streets I visited,
Blazed with you possible; other voices bred
Yours in my quick ear; when the rain was cold
Shiver it might make shoulders I behold
Sloping through kite-slipt hours, tingling. I said
A month since, 'I will see that cloud-gold head,
Those eyes lighten, and go by': then your thunder rolled.

Drowned all sound else, I come driven to learn
Fearful and happy, deafening rumours of
The complete conversations of the angels, now
As nude upon some warm lawn softly turn
Toward me the silences of your breasts . . My vow! . .
One knee unnerves the voyeur sky enough.

[3]

Who for those ages ever without some blood
Plumped for a rose and plucked it through its fence? . .
Till the canny florist, amorist of cents,
Unpawned the peppery apple, making it good
With boredom, back to its branch, as it seems he could,—
Vending the thornless rose. We think our rents
Paid, and we nod. O but ghosts crowd, dense,
Down in the dark shop bare stems with their Should

Not! Should Not sleepwalks where no clocks agree!
So I was not surprised, though I trembled, when
This morning groping your hand moaning your name
I heard distinctly drip . . somewhere . . and see
Coiled in our joys flicker a tongue again,
The fall of your hair a cascade of white flame.

Ah when you drift hover before you kiss
More my mouth yours now, lips grow more to mine
Teeth click, suddenly your tongue like a mulled wine
Slides fire,—I wonder what the point of life is.
Do, down this night when I adore you, Lise,
So I forsake the blest assistant shine
Of deep-laid maps I made for summits, swine-
enchanted lover, loafing in the abyss?

Loaf hardly, while my nerves dance, while the gale
Moans like your hair down here. But I lie still,
Strengthless and smiling under a maenad rule.
Whose limbs worked once, whose imagination's grail
Many or some would nourish, must now I fill
My strength with desire, my cup with your tongue,
    no more Melpomene's, but Erato's fool? . .

The poet hunched, so, whom the worlds admire,
Rising as I came in; greeted me mildly,
Folded again, and our discourse was easy,
While he hid in his skin taut as a wire,
Considerate as grace, a candid pyre
Flaring some midday shore; he took more tea,
I lit his cigarette . . once I lit Yeats' as he
Muttered before an Athenaeum fire
The day Dylan had tried to slow me drunk
Down to the great man's club. But you laught just now
Letting me out, you bubbled 'Liar' and
Laught . . Well, but thén my breast was empty, monk
Of Yeatsian order: yesterday (truth now)
Flooding blurred Eliot's words sometimes,
    face not your face, hair not you blonde but iron.

Rackman and victim grind: sounds all these weeks
Of seconds and hours and days not once are dumb,
And has your footfall really not come
Still? O interminable strength that leaks
All day away alert . . I am who seeks
As tautly now, whom the vague creakings strum
Jangled this instant, as when the monstrous hum
Your note began!—since when old silence spéaks.

Deep down this building do I sometimes hear
Below the sighs and flex of the travelling world
Pyromaniacal whispers? . . *Not to be*
They say *would do us good* . . easy . . the mere
Lick and a promise of a sweet flame curled
Fast on its wooden love: *silence our plea.*

I've found out why, that day, that suicide
From the Empire State falling on someone's car
Troubled you so; and why we quarrelled. War,
Illness, an accident, I can see (you cried)
But not this: what a bastard, not spring wide! . .
I said a man, life in his teeth, could care
Not much just whom he spat it on . . and far
Beyond my laugh we argued either side.

'One has a right not to be fallen on! . .'
(Our second meeting . . yellow you were wearing.)
Voices of our resistance and desire!
Did I divine then I must shortly run
Crazy with need to fall on you, despairing?
Did you bolt so, before it caught, our fire?

College of flunkeys, and a few gentlemen,
Of whippersnappers and certain serious boys,
Who better discriminates than I your noise
From the lemon song and black light assertion
Of the academies of eternity? . . Your fen—
Yet it's your fen yields this perfume I poise
Full against Helen, and Isotta: toys
To time's late action in this girl. Again
As first when I sat down amongst your trees
I respect you and am moved by you! Hér you
Taught not, nor could, but comrades of hers you have,
She sleeps, she rouses, near you, near she frees
Each morning her strange eyes, eyes that grey blue
Not blue . . for your incurable sins some salve.

Great citadels whereon the gold sun falls
Miss you O Lise sequestered to the West
Which wears you Mayday lily at its breast,
Part and not part, proper to balls and brawls,
Plains, cities, or the yellow shore, not false
Anywhere, free, native and Danishest
Profane and elegant flower,—whom suggest
Frail and not frail, blond rocks and madrigals.

Once in the car (cave of our radical love)
Your darker hair I saw than golden hair
Above your thighs whiter than white-gold hair,
And where the dashboard lit faintly your least
Enlarged scene, O the midnight bloomed . . the East
Less gorgeous, wearing you like a long white glove!

You in your stone home where the sycamore
More than I see you sees you, where luck's grass
Smoothes your bare feet more often, even your glass
Touches your hand and tips to your lips to pour
Whatever is in it into you, through which door
O moving softness do you just now pass—
Your slippers' prows curled, red and old—alas
With what soft thought for me, at sea, and sore?

Stone of our situation, iron and stone,
Younger as days to years than the house, yet might
Wé stare as little haggard with time's roil . .
Who in each other's arms have lain—lie—one
Bite like an animal, both do, pause, and bite,
Shudder with joy, kiss . . the broad waters boil!

I expect you from the North. The path winds in
Between the honeysuckle and the pines, among
Poison ivy and small flowerless shrubs,
Across the red-brown needle-bed. I sit
Or smoking pace. A moment since, at six,
Mist wrapped the knoll, but now birds like a gong
Beat, greet the white-gold level shine. Wide-flung
On a thousand greens the late slight rain is gleaming.

A rabbit jumps a shrub. O my quick darling,
Lie torpid so? Cars from the highway whine,
Dawn's trunks against the sun are black. I shiver.
Your hair this fresh wind would—but I am starting.
To what end does this easy and crystal light
Dream on the flat leaves, emerald, and shimmer? . .

Mutinous armed & suicidal grind
Fears on desires, a clutter humps a track,
The body of expectation hangs down slack
Untidy black; my love sweats like a rind;
Parrots are yattering up the cagy mind,
Jerking their circles . . you stood, a week back,
By, I saw your foot with half my eye, I lack
You . . the damned female's yellow head swings blind.

Cageless they'd grapple. O where, whose Martini
Grows sweeter with my torment, wrung on toward
The insomnia of eternity, loud graves!
Hölderlin on his tower sang like the sea
More you adored that day than your harpsichord,
Troubled and drumming, tempting and empty waves.

I lift—lift you five States away your glass,
Wide of this bar you never graced, where none
Ever I know came, where what work is done
Even by these men I know not, where a brass
Police-car sign peers in, wet strange cars pass,
Soiled hangs the rag of day out over this town,
A juke-box brains air where I drink alone,
The spruce barkeep sports a toupee alas—

My glass I lift at six o'clock, my darling,
As you plotted . . Chinese couples shift in bed,
We shared today not even filthy weather,
Beasts in the hills their tigerish love are snarling,
Suddenly they clash, I blow my short ash red,
Grey eyes light! and we have our drink together.

Moths white as ghosts among these hundreds cling
Small in the porchlight . . I am one of yours,
Doomed to a German song's stale metaphors,
The breasty thimble-rigger hums my wring.

I am your ghost, this pale ridiculous thing
Walks while you slump asleep; ouija than morse
Reaches me better; wide on Denmark's moors
I loiter, and when you slide your eyes I swing.

The billiard ball slammed in the kibitzer's mouth
Doctor nor dentist could relieve him of,
Injecting, chipping . . too he clampt it harder . .

Squalor and leech of curiosity's truth
Fork me this diamond meal to gag on love,
Grinning with passion, your astonished martyr.

What was Ashore, then? . . Cargoed with Forget,
My ship runs down a midnight winter storm
Between whirlpool and rock, and my white love's form
Gleams at the wheel, her hair streams. When we met
Seaward, Thought frank & guilty to each oar set
Hands careless of port as of the waters' harm.
Endless a wet wind wears my sail, dark swarm
Endless of sighs and veering hopes, love's fret.

Rain of tears, real, mist of imagined scorn,
No rest accords the fraying shrouds, all thwart
Already with mistakes, foresight so short.
Muffled in capes of waves my clear sighs, torn,
Hitherto most clear,—Loyalty and Art.
And I begin now to despair of port.

(AFTER PETRARCH & WYATT)

Thrice, or I moved to sack, I saw you: how
Without siege laid I can as simply tell
As whether below the dreams of Astrophel
Lurks local truth some scholars would allow
And others will deny in ours! O now
The punishing girl met after Toynbee's bell
Tolled for us all I see too bloody well
To say why then I cheapened a blind bow.

Paid at the shore eyes, ears, a shaking hand,
A pull of blood; behind you coming back,
Already holding, began to be borne away . .
Held. After Mozart, saw you bend and stand
Beside my seat . . held. I recovered. . . Rack
The consumer! I rushed out Rockwell Street one day.

The Old Boys' blazers like a Mardi-Gras
Burn orange, border black, their dominoes
Stagger the green day down the tulip rows
Of the holiday town. Ever I passioned, ah
Ten years, to go where by her golden bra
Some sultry girl is caught, to dip my nose
Or dance where jorums clash and King Rex' hose
Slip as he rules the tantrum's orchestra,
Liriodendron, and the Mystick Krewe!
Those images of Mardi-Gras' sweet weather
Beckoned—but how has their invitation ceased?
. . The bells brawl, calling (I cannot find you
With me there) back us who were not together.
Our forward Lent set in before our feast.

You, Lise, *contrite* I never thought to see,
Whom nothing fazes, no *crise* can disconcert,
Who calm cross crises all year, flouting, alert,
A reckless lady, in whom alone agree
Of bristling states your war and peace; only
Your knuckle broke with smashing objects, curt
Classic dislike, your flowing love, expert
Flat stillness on hot sand, display you wholly.

. . And can you do what you are sorry for? . .
'I'll pin you down and put a biscuit on you'
Your childhood hissed: you didn't: just this side
Idolatry, I cannot see you sor-
ry, darling, no! what other women do
And lie or weep for, flash in your white stride.

You sailed in sky-high, with your speech askew
But marvellous, and talked like mad for hours,
Slamming and blessing; you transported us,
I'd never heard you talk so, and I knew—
Humbler and more proud—you each time undo
My kitcat but to cram it with these powers
You bare and bury; suddenly, late then, as
Your best 'burnt offering' took me back with you.

No jest but jostles truth! . . I burn . . am led
Burning to slaughter, passion like a sieve
Disbands my circling blood the priestess slights.
—'Remorse does not suit you at all' he said,
Rightly; but what he ragged, and might forgive,
I shook for, lawless, empty, without rights.

Presidential flags! and the General is here,
Shops have let out, two bands are raising hell
O hell is empty and Knowlton Street is well,
The little devils shriek, an angelic tear
Falls somewhere, so (but I laugh) would mine, I fear
The Secret Service rang the rising bell
And poor Mr Eliot and the Admiral
Have come, and a damned word nobody can hear.

Two centuries here have been abused our youth:
(Your grey eyes pierce the miles to meet my eyes)
The bicentennial of an affair with truth
(In the southern noon whom do you tyrannize?)
Not turned out well: the cast girl sucks her tooth.
(Secret, let us be true time crucifies.)

Whom undone David into the dire van sent
I'd see as far. I can't dislike that man,
Grievously and intensely like him even,
Envy nor jealousy admit, consent
Neither to the night of rustlers I frequent
Nor to this illness dreams them; but I can,
Only, that which we must: bright as a pan
Our love gleams, empty almost empty—lent.

. . Did he, or not, see? I stood close to you
But our lips had broken and you could reply . .
And *is* he clement? does he give us rope?
It is the owner drives one crazy, who
Came, or luck brought him, first; a police spy;
A kind and good man; with a gun; hunts hope.

If not white shorts—then in a princess gown
Where gaslights pierce the mist I'd have your age,
Young in a grey gown, blonde and royal, rage
Of handlebars at Reisenweber's, frown
Or smile to quell or rally half the town,
To polka partners mad, to flout the stage,
To pale The Lily to an average
Woman, looking up from your champagne, or down.

Myself, ascotted, still dumb as a mome
Drinking your eyes . . No Bill comes by to cadge
A Scotch in Rector's, waving his loose tongue.
I tip my skimmer to your friend who clung
Too long, blue-stocking cracked on the *Red Badge*
Stevie's becoming known for . . We drive home.

They may suppose, because I would not cloy your ear—
If ever these songs by other ears are heard—
With 'love' and 'love', I loved you not, but blurred
Lust with strange images, warm, not quite sincere,
To switch a bedroom black. O mutineer
With me against these empty captains! gird
Your scorn again above all at *this* word
Pompous and vague on the stump of his career.

Also I fox 'heart', striking a modern breast
Hollow as a drum, and 'beauty' I taboo;
I want a verse fresh as a bubble breaks,
As little false. . . Blood of my sweet unrest
Runs all the same—I am in love with you—
Trapped in my rib-cage something throes and aches!

Still it pleads and rankles: 'Why do you love *me?*'
Replies then jammed me dumb; but now I speak,
Singing why each should *not* the other seek—
The octet will be weaker—in the fishful sea.
Your friends I don't like all, and poetry
You less than music stir to, the blue streak
Troubles me you drink: if all these are weak
Objections, they are all, and all I foresee.

Your choice, though! . . Who no Goliath has slung low.
When one day rushing about your lawn you saw
Him whom I might not name without some awe
If curious Johnson should enquire below,
'Who lifts this voice harsh, fresh, and beautiful?'
—'As thy soul liveth, O king, I cannot tell.'

Sometimes the night echoes to prideless wailing
Low as I hunch home late and fever-tired,
Near you not, nearing the sharer I desired,
Toward whom till now I sailed back; but that sailing
Yaws, from the cabin orders like a failing
Dribble, the stores disordered and then fired
Skid wild, the men are glaring, the mate has wired
Hopeless: locked in, and humming, the Captain's nailing
A false log to the lurching table. Lies
And passion sing in the cabin on the voyage home,
The burgee should fly Jolly Roger: wind
Madness like the tackle of a crane (outcries
Ascend) around to heave him from the foam
Irresponsible, since all the stars rain blind.

Crouched on a low ridge sloping to where you pour
No doubt a new drink late this easy night,
The tooth-drawn town dreams . . censorless, can bite
Rebellion, bodies mauled . . but breaks a snore.
Hessians maraud no more, coaches no more
Crash off north, south; only a smooth car's flight
Hums where the brains rest, an old parasite
Sniff then for breakfast while from Bach you soar

Easy and live in the summer dawn, my striker!
Nothing the borough lets be made here, lest
The professors and the millionaires from bed
Be startled, the Negroes drop trays, build. The tiger
Sprang off heraldic colours into the West,
Where he snoozes . . glossy, and substantially dead.

In a poem made by Cummings, long since, his
Girl was the rain, but darling you are sunlight
Volleying down blue air, waking a flight
Of sighs to follow like the mourning iris
Your shining-out-of-shadow hair I miss
A fortnight and to-noon. What you excite
You are, you are me: as light's parasite
For vision on . . us. O if my syncrisis
Teases you, briefer than Propertius' in
This paraphrase by Pound—to whom I owe
Three letters—why, run through me like a comb:
I lie down flat! under your discipline
I die. No doubt of visored others, though . .
The broad sky dumb with stars shadows me home.

A wasp skims nearby up the bright warm air,
Immobile me, my poem of you lost
Into your image burning, a burning ghost
Between the bricks and fixed eyes, blue despair
To spell you lively in this summerfare
Back from your death of distance, my lute tossed
Down, while my ears reel to your marriage, crossed
Brass endless, burning on my helpless glare.

After eighteen years to the Rue Fortunée
Balzac brought Hanska, the Count dead and the lover
Not well to live, home, where the black lock stuck
Stuck! stuck! lights blazed, the crazy valet smashed away,
Idlers assembled, a smith ran to discover—
Ten weeks, and then turned in (like mine) his luck.

The cold rewards trail in, when the man is blind
They glitter round his tomb (no bivouac):
The Rue Fortunée is the Rue de Balzac,
The Bach-Gesellschaft girdles the world; unsigned,
The treaty rages freeing him to wind
Mankind about an icy finger. Pack
His laurel in, startle him with gimcrack
Recognition.—But O do not remind
Of the hours of morning this indifferent man
When alone in a summery cloud he sweat and knew
She, she would not come, she would not come, now
Or all the lime-slow day. . . Your artisan
And men's, I tarry alike for fame and you,
Not hoping, tame, tapping my warm blank brow.

Of all that weeks-long day, though call it back
If I will I can—rain thrice, sheets, a torrent
Spaced by the dry sun, Sunday thirst that went
Sharp-set from town to town, down cul-de-sac
To smoke a blind pig for a liquid snack,
Did ever beer taste better, when opulent
Over the State line with the State's consent
We cleared our four throats, climbing off the rack;
Lost our way then: our thirst again: then tea
With a velvet jacket over the flowered choker
Almost a man, who copied tulips *queerer:*
Dinner a triumph—of that day I have wholly
One moment (weeks I played the friendly joker)
Your eyes married to mine in the car mirror.

Troubling are masks . . the faces of friends, my face
Met unawares and your face: where I mum
Your doubleganger writhes, wraiths are we come
To keep a festival, none but wraiths embrace;
Our loyal rite only we interlace,
Laertes' winding-sheet done and undone
In Ithaca by day and night . . we thrum
Hopeful our shuffles, trusting to our disgrace.

Impostors . . O but our truth our fortunes cup
To flash this lying blood. Sore and austere
The crown we cry for, merely to lie ill
In grand evasion, questions *not come up*.—
I am dreaming on the hour when I can hear
My last lie rattle, and then lie truly still.

How can I sing, western & dry & thin,
You who for celebration should cause flow
The sensual fanfare of D'Annunzio,
Mozart's mischievous joy, the amaranthine
Mild quirks of Marvell, Villon sharp as tin
Solid as sword-death when the man blinks slow
And accordions into the form he'll know
Forever—voices can nearly make me sin
With envy, so they sound. You they saw not,
Natheless, alas, unto this epigone
Descends the dread labour, the Olympic hour—
When for the garden and the tape of what
We trust, one runs until lung into bone
Hardens, runs harder then . . lucky, a flower.

Audacities and fêtes of the drunken weeks!
One step false pitches all down . . come and pour
Another . . Strange, warningless we four
Locked, crocked together, two of us made sneaks—
Who can't get at each other—midnights of freaks
On crepitant surfaces, a kiss blind from the door . .
One head suspects, drooping and vaguely sore,
Something entirely sad, skew, she not seeks . .

'You'll give me ulcers if all this keeps up'
You moaned . . One only, ignorant and kind,
Saves his own life useful and usual,
Blind to the witch-antinomy I sup
Spinning between the laws on the black edge, blind
Head—O do I?—I dance to disannul.

'I *couldn't leave* you' you confessed next day.
Our law too binds. Grossly however bound
And jacketed apart, ensample-wound,
We come so little and can so little stay
Together, what can we know? Anything may
Amaze me: this did. Ah, to work underground
Slowly and wholly in your vein profound . .
Or like some outcast ancient Jew to say:

'There *is* Judaea: in it Jerusalem:
In that the Temple: in the Temple's inmost
Holy of holies hides the invisible Ark—
There nothing—there all—vast wing beating dark—
Voiceless, the terrible I AM—the lost
Tables of stone with the Law graved on them!'

Nothing there? nothing up the sky alive,
Invisibly considering? . . I wonder.
Sometimes I heard Him in traditional thunder;
Sometimes in sweet rain, or in a great 'plane, I've
Concluded that I heard Him not. You thrive
So, where I pine. See no adjustment blunder?
Job was alone with Satan? Job? O under
Hell-ladled morning, some of my hopes revive:

. . Less nakedly malign—loblolly—dull
Eyes on our end . . a table crumples, things
Jump and fuse, a fat voice calls down the sky,
'Too excitable! too sensitive! thin-skull,
I am for you: I shrive your wanderings:
Stand closer, evil, till I pluck your sigh.'

Keep your eyes open when you kiss: do: when
You kiss. All silly time else, close them to;
Unsleeping, I implore you (dear) pursue
In darkness me, as I do you again
Instantly we part . . only me both then
And when your fingers fall, let there be two
Only, 'in that dream-kingdom': I would have you
Me alone recognize your citizen.

Before who wanted eyes, making love, so?
I do now. However we are driven and hide,
What state we keep all other states condemn,
We see ourselves, we watch the solemn glow
Of empty courts we kiss in . . Open wide!
You do, you do, and I look into them.

Sigh as it ends . . . I keep an eye on your
Amour with Scotch,—too *cher* to consummate;
Faster your disappearing beer than late-
ly mine; your naked passion for the floor;
Your hollow leg; your hanker for one more
Dark as the Sundam Trench; how you dilate
Upon psychotics of this class, collate
Stages, and . . how long since you, well, *forbore.*

Ah, but the high fire sings on to be fed
Whipping our darkness by the lifting sea
A while, O darling drinking like a clock.
The tide comes on: spare, Time, from what you spread
Her story,—tilting a frozen Daiquiri,
Blonde, barefoot, beautiful,
    flat on the bare floor rivetted to Bach.

Musculatures and skulls. Later some throng
Before a colonnade, eagle on goose
Clampt in an empty sky, time's mild abuse
In cracks clear down the fresco print; among
The exaggeration of poses and the long
Dogged perspective, difficult to choose
The half-forgotten painter's lost excuse:
A vanished poet crowned by the Duke for song.

Yours crownless, though he keep four hundred years
To be mocked so, will not be sorry if
Some of you keeps, grey eyes, your dulcet lust . .
So the old fiction fools us on, Hope steers
Rather us lickerish towards some hieroglyph
Than whelms us home, loinless and sleepy dust.

And does the old wound shudder open? Shall
I nurse again my days to a girl's sight,
Feeling the bandaged and unquiet night
Slide? Writhe in silly ecstasy? Banal
Greetings rehearse till a quotidian drawl
Carols a promise? Stoop an acolyte
Who stood my master? Must my blood flow bright,
Childish, I chilled and darkened? Strong pulse crawl?

I see I do, it must, trembling I see
Grace of her switching walk away from me
Fastens me where I stop now, smiling pain;
And neither pride don nor the fever shed
More, till the *furor* when we slide to bed,
Trying calenture for the raving brain.

Marble nor monuments whereof then we spoke
We speak of more; spasmodic as the wasp
About my windowpane, our short songs rasp—
Not those alone before their singers choke—
Our sweetest; none hopes now with one smart stroke
Or whittling years to crack away the hasp
Across the ticking future; all our grasp
Cannot beyond the butt secure its smoke.

A Renaissance fashion, not to be recalled.
We dinch 'eternal numbers' and go out.
We understand exactly what we are.
. . Do we? Argent I craft you as the star
Of flower-shut evening: who stays on to doubt
I sang true? ganger with trobador and scald!

And Plough-month peters out . . its thermal power
Squandered in sighs and poems and hopeless thought,
Which corn and honey, wine, soap, wax, oil ought
Upon my farmling to have chivvied into flower.
I burn, not silly with remorse, in sour
Flat heat of the dying month I stretch out taut:
Twenty-four dawns the topaz woman wrought
To smile to me is gone. These days devour
Memory: what were you elbowed on your side?
Supine, your knee flexed? do I hear your words
Faint as a nixe, in our grove, saying farewells? . .
At five I get up sleepless to decide
What I will not today do; ride out: hear birds
Antiphonal at the dayspring, and nothing else.

The clots of age, grovel and palsy, crave
Mádmen: to gasp, unreasonably weep,
Gravid with ice, staving invincible sleep. . .
Still as I watch this two tonight I waive
Half of my fear, envy sues even: grave,
Easy and light with juniors, he, and steep
In his honours she, beloved, wholly they keep
Together, accustomed; hircine excitement gave
No joy so deep, and died . . Fill my eyes with tears,
I stare down the intolerable years
To the mild survival—where, you are where, where?
'I *want* to take you for my lover' just
You vowed when on the way I met you: must
Then that be all (*Do*) the shorn time we share?

You should be gone in winter, that Nature mourn
With me your anarch separation, call-
ing warmth all with you: as more poetical
Than to be left biting the dog-days, lorn
Alone when all else burgeons, brides are born,
Children yet (some) begotten, every wall
Clasped by its vine here . . crony alcohol
Comfort as random as the unicorn.

Listen, for poets are feigned to lie, and I
For you a liar am a thousand times,
Scars of these months blazon like a decree:
I would have you—a liner pulls the sky—
Trust when I mumble me. Than gin-&-limes
You are cooler, darling, O come back to me.

Bell to sore knees vestigial crowds, let crush
One another nations sottish and a-prowl,
Talon the Norway rat to a barn owl
At wind-soft midnight; split the sleepy hush
With sirens; card-hells create; from a tower push
The frantic hesitator; strike a rowel
To a sad nag; probe, while they whiten & howl,
With rubber gloves the prisoners' genial slush;

Enact our hammer time; only from time
Twitch while the wind works my beloved and me
Once with indulgent tongs for a little free,—
Days, deer-fleet years, to be a paradigm
For runaways and the régime's exiles.
. . The wind lifts, soon, the cold wind reconciles.

Boy twenty-one, in Donne, shied like a blow,—
His prose, from poems' seductive dynamite,—
I read 'The adulterer waits for the twilight . .
The twilight comes, and serves his turn.' (Not so:
Midnight or dawn.) I stuttered frightened 'No,
Nóne could decline, crookt, ghastly, from the sight
Of elected love and love's delicious rite
Upon the livid stranger Loves forego.'

. . I am this strange thing I despised; you are.
To become ourselves we are these wayward things.
And the lies at noon, months' tremblings, who foresaw?
And I did not foresee fraud of the Law
The scarecrow restraining like a man, its rings
Blank . . my love's eyes familiar as a scar!

Are we? You murmur 'not'. What of the night
Attack on the dark road we could not contain, ⌐
Twice I slid to you sudden as the stain
Joy bloods the wanderer at the water's sight,
And back, but you writhed on me . . as I write
I tremble . . trust me not to keep on sane
Until you whisper 'Come to me again'
Unless you whisper soon. O come we soon
Together dark and sack each other outright,
Doomed cities loose and thirsty as a dune . .
Lovers we are, whom now the on-tide licks.
Our fast of famed sleep stirs, darling, diurnal,—
Hurry! till we, beginning our eternal
Junket on the winds, wake like a ton of Styx.

How far upon these songs with my strict wrist
Hard to bear down, who knows? None is to read
But you: so gently . . but then truth's to heed,
The sole word, near or far, shot in the mist.

Double I sing, I must, your utraquist,
Crumpling a syntax at a sudden need,
Stridor of English softening to plead
O to you plainly lest you more resist.

'Arthur lay then at Caerlon upon Usk . .'
I see, and all that story swims back . . red
Satin over rushes . . Mother's voice at dusk.

So I comb times and men to cram you rare:
'Faire looketh *Ceres* with her yellow Haire'—
Fairer you far O here lie filteréd.

I've met your friend at last, your violent friend,
Laughter out of a hard life; and she out,
Treating in talk one door really as shut
That should be shut, gashes will hardly mend.
'Here is Katrina' at the other end
Of telephones . . 'Heck, I feel wonderful! . .'
And so do I when I am with her, but
I would she knew she lashed me where I bend.

And so do I when I am with her, only
Her 'they' and 'harmony' harry me lone and wild.
. . How she loves you! and then to disarrange,
Powerful chemist, all the years she's filed
With stubborn work, for the law! . . she means to change.
So do I mean,—less (when I rise up) lonely.

One note, a daisy, and a photograph,
To slake this siege of weeks without you, all.
Your dawn-eyed envoy, welcome as Seconal,
To call you faithful . . now this cenotaph,
A shabby mummy flower. Note I keep safe,
Nothing, on a ration slip a social scrawl—
Not that it didn't forth some pages call
Of my analysis, one grim paragraph.

The snapshot then—your eyes down, your hair bound:
Your power leashed, but too your blaze is dim . .
By the sea, thinking, long before we met;
Akimbo from your nape, what petrels round
(Out of the print) your unsuspicious slim
Dear figure, warning 'Dream of him
    now you not know whom you will not forget.'

They come too thick, hail-hard, and all beside
Batter, necessities of my nights and days,
My proper labour that my storm betrays
Weekly lamented, weakly flung aside;
What in the musical wind to work but glide
Among the wind, willing my eyes should daze
Fast on her image, for an exhaustless phrase,
While themes throng, the rapt world one & hers & wide.

They crowd on, crowning what I perforce complain
Remorseful in my journal of, and lest
Thick they fall thin, I beg the calm belongs,—
Traditional meditation. But when my rein
Fails most, still I race feeble to protest
These two months . . decades of excited songs.

A tongue there is wags, down in the dark wood O:
Trust it not. It trills malice among friends,
Irrelevant squibs and lies, to its own ends
Or to no ends, simply because it would O.
To us, us most I hear, it prinks no good O;
Has its idea, Jamesian; apprehends
Truth non-aviarian; meddles, and 'defends'
Honour free . . that such a bill so wily should O!

Who to my hand all year flew to be fed
Makes up his doubts to dart at us . . Ah well,
Did you see the *green* of that catalpa tree?—
A certain jackal will lose half its head
For cheek, our keek, our hairy philomel.—
How can you tell?—A little bird told me.

A sullen brook hardly would satisfy
The Winter-traveller slumps near, Stony Brook;
Prattle of brooks it scorns, only in some crook
Fetches again and now a muddy sigh
Reaches me here.—A liner rocks the sky,
I shudder beneath the trees. I brought a book,
Shut on my brown knee. Once I rise and look
Under the bridge-arch. The third day of July.

Close, going back, I pass (still as a mouse)
The fatuous stranger in the stone strong home
Now you and my friend your husband are away.
And I must gnaw there somewhy. Double day:
In the end I race by cocky as a comb,
Adust . . *Da ist meiner Liebstens Haus.*

Some sketch sweat' out, unwilling swift & crude,
A hundred more like bats in swelter-day
A-lunge about my office, I'm away
Downstairs for coffee, and to rest, and brood.
. . The *mots* fly, and the flies mope on the food
Where all-age adolescents swig and bray,
An ice-cream-soda jag, the booths are gay . .
The ass-eyes after me unlid, protrude.

And I have fled antcrazy to my task
In the hotbox at the top of Upper Wyne
To work their children music! as ice cubes
Pleasing, colder keeping, more than they ask,
As worthy of them—not of you . . No sign . .
Ermite-amateur in the midst of the boobs.

It was the sky all day I grew to and saw.
I cycled southeast through the empty towns,
Flags hanging out, between the summer grains,
Meeting mainly the azure minions of our law.

Near our fake lake an artificial pool
Was full of men and women; all the rest,
Shore for the Fourth. I crookt two roses. Most
I studied the sky's involuntary rule.

I followed a cloud and finally I caught it,
Springing my ribbon down the world of green . .
Shadow to shadow, under tropical day . .

Flat country, slow, alone. So in my pocket
Your snapshot nightmares where (cloth, flesh between)
My heart was, before I gave it away.

When I recall I could believe you'd go
I start. I can't believe you will come back.
Months on to Monday, and then Monday's rack
Uncertain up the sky unseen winds blow
Bringing what weather I cannot foreknow.
Still I see better in my almanac
Your coming, than in the columns white & black
My going later. All our plans outgrow
My local eyes, locked where somehow we draw
Somewhat together, wince to a single goad,
Each other steady . . steadily closer . . keep.
Closer: against the departures of our law
Let's Dido-like 'forge causes of abode' . .
Whom the sliding stars wheedle as one to sleep.

Sunderings and luxations, *luxe*, and grief-
unending exile from the original spouse,
Dog-fights! one bites intimate as a louse
The lousy other, Love the twitching leaf
Wide to the weather, hangover-long, jag-brief,
Nulliparous intensities, or as mouse
To cats the child to broken parents, house
Sold, books divided . . divorce as a relief . .

We discussed, drinking, one sad afternoon
In a Connecticut house in cloudy June,
Thinking, whoever was mentioned, still of others.
I thought of you,—come we too to this vile
Loose fagend? earlier *still* loves so defile? . .
Could *our* incredible marriage . . like all others' . . ?

Our love conducted as in heavy rain
Develops hair and lowers its head: the lash
And weight of rain breed, like the soundless slosh
Divers make round a wrack, régime, domain
Invisible, to us inured invisible stain
Of all our process; also lightning flash
Limns us audacious and furtive, whom slow crash
On crash jolt like the mud- and storm-blind Wain.

If the rain ceased and the unlikely sun
Shone out! . . whom our stars shake, could we emerge
Trustful and clear into the common rank,—
So long deceiving?—Days when Dathan sank
Quick to the pit not past, darling, we verge
Daily O there: have strange changes begun?

Sensible, coarse, and moral; in decent brown;
Its money doling to an orphanage;
Sober . . well-spirited but sober; sage
Plain nourishing life nor you nor I could down
I doubt, our blinkers lost, blood like a clown
Dancing upon a one-night hot-foot stage,
Brains in a high wind, high brains, the next page
Trembling,—the water's fine, come in and drown.

Since the corruption of the working classes
I am speaking of the Eighteenth Century: kisses
Opening on betrothals, love like a vise.
Where shawm and flute flutter the twilight, where
Conjugal, toothless, has a booth at the Fair,
The Reno brothels boom, suddenly we writhe.

Loves are the summer's. Summer like a bee
Sucks our best off, thigh-brushes, and is gone.
The yellow pollen upon the white winds blown
Settles. I feel the summer draining me,
I lean back breathless in an agony
Of charming loss I suffer without moan,
Without my love, or with my love alone.
She left me in the Spring, or I say wé

Left before there we bloomed our secret garden!
The ghosts of breezes widowy small paths wander,
A fruitless bird pipes its surprising sorrow.
When will she, she come back? . . against whom I harden
My effortless ghost in vain, who moved asunder
Flowers at the come of summer beautiful and narrow.

Today is it? Is it today? I shudder
For nothing in my chair, and suddenly yawn.
Today I suddenly believe. Since dawn
When I got up, my muscles like a rudder
Strain crosswise from this work. I rise and mutter
Something, and hum, pace, and sit down again
Hard. A butterfly in my shoulder then
Stops and aches. My stomach swings like a shutter.

As the undergrounds piston a force of air
Before their crash into the station, you
Are felt before your coming, and the platforms shake.
So light, so small, so far still, to impair
Action and peace so . . risks we take make true
Maybe our safeties . . *come* for our risk's sake.

Languid the songs I wish I willed . . I try . .
Smooth songs untroubled like a silver spoon
To pour your creamy beauty back, warm croon
Blind, soft . . but I have something in my eye,
I see by fits, see what there, rapid and sly,
Difficult, so that it will be off soon,
I'd better *fix* it! frantic as a loon,
Smarting, world-churned, some convulsed song I cry.

Well . . (also I plead, I have something in mind,
My bobsled need, the need for me you'll find
If you look deeper: study our winter-scene) . .
Thinking is well, but worse still to be caught
The wholly beautiful just beyond thought,—
Small trees in mist far down an endless green!

Tyranny of your car—so much resembles
Beachwagons all, all with officious hope
Conscript my silly eyes—offers a trope
For your grand sway upon these months my shambles:
Your cleaver now to other women's brambles
I'll not contrast—no, all of you have scope,
Teeth breasts tongues thighs eyes hair: as rope to rope
You point to point compare, and the subject trembles.

What makes yóu then this ominous wide blade
I'd run from O unless I bleat to die?
Nothing: you are not: woman blonde, called Lise.
It is I lope to be your sheep, to wade
Thick in my cordial blood, to howl and sigh
As I decide . . if I could credit this.

Here too you came and sat a time once, drinking.
I could have cut their throats to be alone.
Yet all the hour I slumped here like a stone
My heart smiled, I smiled while my heart was sinking.
Happier than I seemed for their hoodwinking,
My smile was under . . over . . so was the moan
Arcane I kept out of the 'master' tone
Native to me I adopted . . my rabid thinking.

Juggler and cull! and places, words, call up
Inscrutable disturbance bound to you
Partout! partout some crowning or some crime;
As Julian spending a nickel, Wid a dime,
Mazes of instant silence must pursue,—
Obsession's hypocrites, time's, their own dupe.

The dew is drying fast, a last drop glistens
White on a damaged leaf not far from me.
A pine-cone calmed here in a red-brown sea
Collects its straying forces now and listens:
A veery calls; south, a slow whistle loosens
My lone control. The flat sun finally
Flaws through the evergreen grove, and can be he—
If Lise comes—our renewed love lights and christens.

Tarry today? . . weeks the abandoned knoll
And I have waited. The needles are soft . . feel.
The village bell, or the college, tells me seven.
Much longer not sustains—will it again?—
Castaway time I scrabble tooth and nail,
I crush a cigarette black, and go down.

Once when they found me, some refrain '*Quoi faire?*'
Striking my hands, they say repeatedly
I muttered; although I could hear and see
I knew no one.—I am silent in my chair,
And stronger and more cold is my despair
At last, for I have come into a country
Whose vivid Queen upon no melody
Admits me. *Manchmal glaub ich, ich kann nicht mehr.*

Song follows song, the chatterer to the fire
Would follow soon . . Deep in Ur's royal pits
Sit still the courtly bodies, a little bowl
By each, attired to voluntary blitz . .
In Shub-ad's grave the fingers of a girl
Were touching still, when they found her, the strings of
    her lyre.

Astronomies and slangs to find you, dear,
Star, art-breath, crowner, conscience! and to chart
For kids unborn your distal beauty, part
On part that startles, till you blaze more clear
And witching than your sister Venus here
To a late age can, though her senior start
Is my new insomnia,—swift sleepless art
To draw you even . . and to draw you near.

I prod our English: cough me up a word,
Slip me an epithet will justify
My daring fondle, fumble of far fire
Crackling nearby, unreasonable as a surd,
A flash of light, an insight: I am the shy
Vehicle of your cadmium shine . . your choir.

Faith like the warrior ant swarming, enslaving
Or griding others, you gave me soft as dew,
My darling, drawing me suddenly into you,
Your arms' strong kindness at my back, your weaving
Thighs agile to me, white teeth in your heaving
Hard, your face bright and dark, back, as we screw
Our lives together—twin convulsion—blue
Crests curl, to rest . . again the ivy waving.

Faiths other fall. Afterwards I kissed you
So (Lise) long, and your eyes so waxed, marine,
Wider I drowned . . light to their surface drawn
Down met the wild light (derelict weeks I missed you
Leave me forever) upstreaming; never-seen,
Your radiant glad soul surfaced in the dawn.

Where the lane from the highway swerves the first drops fell
Like lead, I bowed my head and drifted up.
Now in the grove they pat like footsteps, but
Not hers, Despair's. In slant lines sentinel
Silver and thin, it rains so into Hell,
Unvisited these thousand years. I grope
A little in the wind after a hope
For sun before she wakes . . all might be well.

All might yet be well . . I wandered just
Down to the upper lane now, the sky was clearing,
And as I scrawl, the sun breaks. Ah, what use?
She said if rain, *no,*—in vain self-abuse
I lie a fairy well! cloud disappearing
Not lonelier, leaving like me: we must.

For you am I collared O to quit my dear
My sandy-haired mild good and most beautiful
Most helpless and devoted wife? I pull
Crazy away from this; but too from her
Resistlessly I draw off, months have, far
And quarrelling—irrelation—numb and dull
Dead Sea with tiny aits . . Love at the full
Had wavered, seeing, foresuffering us here.

Unhappy all her lone strange life until
Somehow I friended it. And the Master catches
Me strongly from behind, and clucks, and tugs.
He has, has he? my heart-relucting will.
She spins on silent and the needle scratches.
—This all, Lise? and stark kisses, stealthy hugs?

Under Scorpion both, back in the Sooner State
Where the dry winds winnow the soul, we both were born,
And we have cast our origin, and the Horn
Neither has frankly scanted, others imitate
Us; and we have come a long way, late
For depth enough, betimes enough for torn
Hangnails of nerves and innocent love, we turn
Together in this vize lips, eyes, our Fate.

When the cam slid, the prodigious fingers tightened
And we began to fuse, weird afternoon
Early in May (the Third), we both were frightened;
A month we writhed, in sudden love like a scrimmage;
June's wide loss worse; the fortnight after June
Worst. Vize and woe worked us this perfect image!

Our Sunday morning when dawn-priests were applying
Wafer and wine to the human wound, we laid
Ourselves to cure ourselves down: I'm afraid
Our vestments wanted, but Francis' friends were crying
In the nave of pines, sun-satisfied, and flying
Subtle as angels about the barricade
Boughs made over us, deep in a bed half made
Needle-soft, half the sea of our simultaneous dying.

'Death is the mother of beauty.' Awry no leaf
Shivering with delight, we die to be well . .
Careless with sleepy love, so long unloving.
What if our convalescence must be brief
As we are, the matin meet the passing bell? . .
About our pines our sister, wind, is moving.

A Cambridge friend put in,—one whom I used
To pay small rope at chess to, who in vain
Luffed up to free a rook,—and through the strain
Of ten-year-old talk cocktails partly loosed
I forgot you, forgot you, for the first
Hour in months of watches . . Mozart's pain
I heard then, in the cranny of the hurricane,
As since the chrisom caught me up immersed

I have heard nothing but the sough of the sea
And wide upon the open sea my friend
The sea-wind crying, out of its cave to roam
No more, no more . . until my memory
Swung you back like a lock: I sing the end,
Tolerant Aeolus to call me home.

Demand me again what Kafka's riddles mean,
For I am the penal colony's prime scribe:
From solitary, firing against the tribe
Uncanny judgments ancient and unclean.
I am the officer flat on my own machine,
Priest of the one Law no despair can bribe,
On whom the mort-prongs hover to inscribe
'I FELL IN LOVE' . . O none of this foreseen,
Adulteries and divorces cold I judged
And strapped the tramps flat. Now the harrow trembles
Down, a strap snaps, I wave—out of control—
To you to change the legend has not budged
These years: make the machine grave on me (stumbles
Someone to latch the strap) 'I MET MY SOUL'.

All I did wrong, all the Grand Guignol years,
Tossed me here still able to touch you still.
I took the false turn on the fantastic hill
Continually, until the top appears.
Even my blind (last night) disordered tears
Conducted me to-morning. When I grew ill
Two years, I only taxed my doctors' skill
To pass me to you fixed . . The damned sky clears
Into a decent sun (this week's the worst
Ever I see-saw) half an hour: this town
My tomb becomes a kind of paradise . .
How then complain? Rain came with a burst,
Ridding the sky. Was it this evil clown
Or surviving lover you called to you? . . *twice.*

18 July

Swarthy when young; who took the tonsure; sign,
His coronation, wangled, his name re-said
For euphony; off to courts fluttered, and fled;
Professorships refused; upon one line
Worked years; and then that genial concubine.
Seventy springs he read, and wrote, and read.
On the day of the year his people found him dead
I read his story. Anew I studied mine.

Also there was Laura and three-seventeen
Sonnets to something like her . . twenty-one years . .
He never touched her. Swirl our crimes and crimes.
Gold-haired (too), dark-eyed, ignorant of rimes
Was she? Virtuous? The old brume seldom clears.
—Two guilty and crepe-yellow months
      Lise! be our bright surviving actual scene.

The two plantations Greatgrandmother brought
My bearded General, back in a world would burn,
I thresh excited as I see return
Odd in this symbol you me last night taught . .
Your Two-fields rapt into the family ought
To save us: sensitivity, elegant, fern-
subtle, knit upon vigour enough to turn
A nation's strong decline. I grind my thought
A bit more, and I bare the quick of the have
And have not, half have, less than half, O this
Fantasy of your gates ajar, gates barred.
Poaching and rack-rent do you hope will save
True to ourselves *us*, darling? owners, Lise!—
Heiress whose lovely holdings lie
    too forkt for truth; called also Kierkegaard.

Fall and rise of her midriff bells. I watch.
Blue knee-long shorts, striped light shirt. Bright between
Copt hills of the cushion a lazy green
Her sun-incomparable face I watch.
A darkness dreams adown her softest crotch,
A hand dreams on her breast, two fingers lean,
The ring shows like a wound. Her hair swirls clean
Alone in the vague room's morning-after botch.

Endymion's Glaucus through a thousand years
Collected the bodies of lovers lost, until
His own beloved's body rustled and sighed . .
So I would, O to spring—blotting her fears,
The others in this house, the house, road, hill—
As once she up the stair sprang to me, lips wide!

On the wheat-sacks, sullen with the ceaseless damp,
William and I sat hours and talked of you,
I talked of you. Potting porter. Just a few
Fireflies were out, no stars, no moon; no lamp.
The Great Dane licked my forearm like a stamp,
Surprisingly, in total darkness. Who
Responds with peaceful gestures, calm and new
This while, your home-strong love's ferocious tramp?

Insonorous and easy night! I lusk,
Until we rise and strike rake-handles in
The nervous sacks to prod and mix with air;
Lest a flame sing out invisible and brusk
About the black barn . . Kingston (and my chin
Sank on the rake-end) suddenly
    I longed for sick, your toxic music there.

I dreamt he drove me back to the asylum
Straight after lunch; we stood then at one end,
A sort of cafeteria behind, my friend
Behind me, nuts in groups about the room;
A dumbwaiter with five shelves was waiting (some-
thing's missing here) to take me up—I bend
And lift a quart of milk to hide and tend,
Take with me. Everybody is watching, dumb.

I try to put it first among some worm-
shot volumes of the N. E. D. I had
On the top shelf —then somewhere else . . slowly
Lise comes up in a matron's uniform
And with a look (I saw once) infinitely sad
In her grey eyes takes it away from me.

Infallible symbolist!—Tanker driven ashore,
An oil-ship by a tropical hurricane
Wrecked on a Delaware beach, the postcard's scene;
On the reverse, words without signature:
Je m'en fiche du monde sans toi—in your
Hand for years busy in the liquid main
To tank you on—your Tulsa father's vein,
Oil. All the worked and wind-slapt waters roar.

O my dear I am sorry, sorry, and glad! and glad
To trope you helpless, there, and needing me,
Where the dangerous land meets the disordered sea . .
Rich on the edge we wait our salvage, sad
And joyous, nervous, that the hired men come
Whom we require, to split us painfully home.

Four oval shadows, paired, ringed each by sun,
The closer smaller pair behind, third pair
Beating symmetrical to the sides in air
Apparently—the water-spiders' dun
Bodies above unlike their shadows run,
Skim with six wires about a black-backed, fair-
bellied and long tube which does not appear
In the atomic drawings on the shallow mud.

My shadow on the vines and water should—
If so it were as Gath in Babylon—
Show a lover's neurons waiting for a letter,
Brook near the postbox, or man's fission's crack
Of comfortable doom. Wé do this better: . .
A solid hypocrite squats there in black.

Why can't, Lise, why shouldn't *they* fall in love?
Mild both, both still in mix of studies, still
Unsteadied into life, novices of the will,
Formed upon others (us), disciples of
The Master and the revisionists: enough
Apart from their attraction, to unstill
The old calm loves (cyclonic loves) until
The electric air shocks them together, rough,
But better in love than grief, who can afford
No storms (ours). Fantasy! . . . Forget.
—I write this leaving Pennsylvania's farms,
Seats 37, 12 Standees, I am tired
Unspeakably of standing: Kiss me, and let
Let me sit down and take you in my arms.

Impossible to speak to her, and worse
To keep on silent, silent hypocrite
Bound for my kindness or my lack of it
Solely to strength you crumple or you nurse
By not being or being with me. Curse
This kindness tricks her to think bit by bit
We *will* be more together . . better . . sit
The poor time out, and then the good rehearse—

When neither my fondness nor my pity can
O no more bend me to Esther with love,
Gladden the sad eyes my lost eyes have seen
With such and so long ache, ah to unman.
When she calls, small, and grieving I must move,
The horror and beauty of your eyes burn between.

How shall I do, to pass the weary time
Of fading entertainments while you're gone?
Early I'll rise still, then from dawn to dawn
To meet you in our grove not once will climb.
Your fingers to my shoulder in some rime
I'll manage only, and your instep drawn
In the morning light remember only; on
Any dropt cue follow you off, and mime

My senseless presence in your presence not,
My comments rather skew—They'll say 'I wonder
What is in Berryman lately? I find him stranger
Than usual'—working their nickel in the slot
They'll try again, dreamless they drag from yonder
Vexed to my leather chair this lathered ranger.

Spendthrift Urethra—Sphincter, frugal one—
Masters from darkness in your double sway
Whom favouring either all chaotic stray—
Adjust us to our love! . . *Unlust* undone,
Wave us together out of the running sun
Suddenly, and rapt from our shore-play,
My loss your consolation and protégé,
Down at a stroke whelmed, while the waters run.

O serious as our play, my nervous plea!
. . Hallucinatory return to the warm and real
Dark, still, happy apartment after the riot . .
Wounded, be well, and sleep sound as the sea
Vexed in wide night by no wind, but the wheel
Roils down to zero . . steady . . archaic quiet.

Our lives before bitterly our mistake!—
We should have been together seething years,
We should have been the tomb-bat hangs and hears
Sounds inconceivable, been a new snowflake,
We should have been the senile world's one sake,
Vestigial lovers, tropical and fierce
Among fatigues and snows, the gangs and queers,
We should have been the bloom of a cockcrow lake.

. . A child's moon, child's fire!—What I love of you
Inter alia tingles like a whole good day,
A hard wind, or a Strad's consummate pluck,
Proficient, full and strong, shrewd as the blue
Profound sky, pale as a winter sky you lay
And with these breasts whiter than stars gave suck.

Is it possible, poor kids, you must not come out?
Care for you none but Lise, to whom you cry?
Here in my small book must you dance, then die?
Rain nor sun greet you first, no friendly shout?
If the army stands, moves not ahead one scout?
Sits all your army ever still, small fry?
And never to all your letters one reply?
No echo back, your games go on without?
Dignity under these conditions few
I feel might muster steadily, and you
Jitterbug more than you pavanne, poor dears . .
Only you seem to want to hunt the whole
House through, scrutators of the difficult soul
Native here—and pomp's not for pioneers.

Anomalous I linger, and ignore
My blue conviction she will now not come
Whose grey eyes blur before me like some sum
A shifting riddle to fatigue . . I pore . .
Faster they flicker, and flag, moving on slower,
And I move with them—who am I? a scum
Thickens on a victim, a delirium
Begins to mutter, which I must explore.

O rapt as Monteverdi's '. . *note* . . *note* . .'
I glide aroused—a rumour? or a dream?
An actual lover? Elmo's light? erlking?
—'I know very well who I am' said Don Quixote.
The sourceless lightning laps my stare, the stream
Backs through the wood, the cosy spiders cling.

'If long enough I sit here, she, she'll pass.'
This fatuous, and suffering-inversion,
And Donne-mimetic, O and true assertion
Tolls through my hypnagogic mind; alas
I hang upon this threshold of plate-glass,
Dry and dull eyes, in the same weird excursion
As from myself our love-months are, some Persian
Or Aztec supersession—the land mass
Extruded first from the archaic sea,
Whereon a desiccation, and species died
Except the one somehow learnt to breathe air:
Unless my lungs adapt me to despair,
I'll nod off into the increasing, wide,
Marvellous sleep my hope lets herald me.

For you an idyl, was it not, so far,
Flowing and inconvulsive pastoral,
I suddenly made out tonight as, all
The pallor of your face lost like a star,
It clenched and darkened in your avatar,
The goddess grounded. Lovers' griefs appal
Women, who with their honey brook their gall
And succor as they can the men they mar.

Down-soft my joy in the beginning, O
Dawn-disenchanted since, I hardly remember
The useful urine-retentive years I sped.
—I said as little as I could, sick; know
Your strange heart works; wish us into September
Only alive, and lovers, and abed.

Itself a lightning-flash ripping the 'dark
Backward' of you-before, you harrowed me
How you and the wild boy (larcener-to-be)
Took horses out one night, full in the stark
Pre-storm midnight blackness, for a lark,
At seventeen, drunk, and you whipt them madly
About the gulph's rim, lightning-split, with glee
About, about. A decade: . . I embark.

How can we know with whom we ride, or soon
Or later, ever? You . . what are yóu like?
A topic's occupied me months, month's mind.
But I more startled may, than who shrank down
And wiped his sharp eyes with a helpless look,
The great tears falling, when Odysseus struck him, find.

What can to you this music wakes my years
(I work you here a wistful specimen)
Be, to you affable and supple, when
The music they call music fills your ears?
Room still? Alive O to my animals' tears?
Haunted by cagy sighs? The cries of men
Versed are you in? Your Tetragrammaton—
Bach, Mozart, Beethoven & Schubert—hears.

No quarrel here once! Pindar sang both sides,—
Two thousand years their easy marriage lasted,
Until some coldness grew . . they moved apart . .
Only one now to rile the other rides
Sometimes, neither will say how he has fasted,
They stare with desire, and spar . . and crib . . and part.

The man who made her let me climb the derrick
At nine (not far from—four—another child)
Produced this steady daring keeps us wild . .
I remember the wind wound on me like a lyric.
One resignation on to more, some cleric
Has told us, helms, would make the Devil mild
At last; one boldness so in the spirit filed
Brings boldness on—collective—atmospheric—

Character in the end, contented on a slope
Brakeless, a nervy ledge . . we overgrow
My derrick into midnights and high dawn,
The riot where I'm happy—still I hope
Sometime to dine with you, sometime to go
Sober to bed, a proper citizen.

Most strange, my change, this nervous interim.—
The utter courtship ended, tokens won,
Assurance salted down . . all this to stun
More than excite: I blink about me grim
And dull and anxious, rather than I skim
Light bright & confident: like a weak pun
I stumble neither way: Hope weighs a ton:
Tired certainly, but much less tired than dim.

—I were absence' adept, a glaring eye;
Or I were agile to this joy, this letter,
You say from Fox Hill: *'I am not the same.'*—
No more am I: I'm neither: without you I
Am not myself. My sight is dying. Better
The searchlights' torture which we overcame!

'Old Smoky' when you sing with Peter, Lise,
Sometimes at night, and your small voices hover
Mother-and-son but sourceless, O yours over
The hesitating treble must be his,
I glide about my metamorphosis
Gently, a tryst of troubled joy—discover
Our pine-grove grown a mountain—the *true* lover
Soft as a flower, hummingbird-piercing, is.

I saw him stretch out farther than a wish
And I have seen him gutted like a fish
At hipshot midnight for you, by your side.—
Last night there in your love-seat, you away,
I sang low to my niece your song, and stray
Still from myself into you singing slide.

It will seem strange, no more this range on range
Of opening hopes and happenings. Strange to be
One's *name* no longer. Not caught up, not free.
Strange, not to wish one's wishes onward. Strange,
The looseness, slopping, time and space estrange.
Strangest, and sad as a blind child, not to see
Ever you, never to hear you, endlessly
Neither you there, nor coming . . Heavy change!—

An instant there is, Sophoclean, true,
When Oedipus must understand: his head—
When Oedipus *believes!*—tilts like a wave,
And will not break, only *ioὺ ioὺ*
Wells from his dreadful mouth, the love he led:
Prolong to Procyon this. This begins my grave.

I say *I laid siege—you enchanted me* . .
Magic and warfare, faithful metaphors
As when their paleolithic woods and tors
The hunter and the witchwife roamed, half free,
Half to the Provider and the Mystery-
riddler bound: the kill, the spell: your languors
I wag my wolf's tail to—without remorse?—
You shudder as I'd pierce you where I knee

l . . Only we little wished, or you to charm
Or I to make you shudder, you to wreck
Or I to hum you daring on my arm.
Abrupt as a dogfight, the air full of
Tails and teeth—the meshing of a trek—
All this began: knock-down-and-drag-out love.

Mallarmé siren upside down,—rootedly!
Dare the top crotch, the utmost two limbs plume
Cloudward, the bole swells just below . . See, from
Her all these leaves and branches! . . world-green . . free
To be herself: firm-subtle-grey-brown barky,
A skin upon her gravest thought: to roam,
Sea-disinclined . . through the round stair I come,
A hollow. Board loose down near your rooftree.

. . I biked out leisurely one day because
My heart was breaking, and swung up with the casual
Passion of May again your sycamore . .
Hand trembling on the top, everything was
Beautiful, inhuman, green and real as usual.—
Your hypocrite hangs on the truth, sea-sore.

A murmuration of the shallow, Crane
Sees us, or so, twittering at nightfall
About the eaves, coloured and houseless soul,
Before the mucksweat rising of the Wain.
No black or white here; and our given brain
Troubles us incompletely; if we call
Sometimes to one another, if we fall
Sorry, we soon forget; wing'd, but in vain.

He fell in love once, when upon her *arms*
He concentrated what I call his faith . .
He died, and dropt into a Jersey hole,
A generation of our culture's swarms
Accumulated honey for your wraith—
Does his wraith watch?—ash-blond and candid soul!

I am interested alone in making ready,
Pointed, more splendid, O the Action which
Attends your whim; bridge interim; enrich
That unimaginable-still, with study
So sharp at time the probe shivers back bloody;
Test the strange circuit but to trust the switch.
The Muse is real, the random shades I stitch—
Devoted vicarage—somewhere real, and steady.

Burnt cork, my leer, my Groucho crouch and rush,
No more my nature than Cyrano's: we
Are 'hindered characters' and mock the time,
The curving and incomprehensible hush
Einstein requires before that colloquy
Altared of joy concludes our pantomime!

Because I'd seen you not believe your lover,
Because you scouted cries come from no cliff,
Because to supplications you were stiff
As Ciro, O as Nero to discover
Slow how your subject loved you, I would hover
Between the slave and rebel—till this life
Arrives:'. . was astonished as I would be if
I leaned against a house and the house fell over . .'

Well, it fell over, over: trust him now:
A stronger house than looked—*you leaned*, and crash,
My walls and ceiling were to be walked on.—
The same thing happened once in Chaplin, how
He solved it now I lose.—Walk on the trash . .
Walk, softly, triste,—little is really gone.

A penny, pity, for the runaway ass!
A nickel for the killer's twenty-six-mile ride!
Ice for the root rut-smouldering inside!
—Eight hundred weeks I have not run to Mass.—
Toss Jack a jawful of good August grass!
'Soul awful,' pray for a soul sometimes has cried!
Wire reasons he seasons should still abide!
—Hide all your arms where he is bound to pass.—

Who drew me first aside? her I forgive,
Or him, as I would be forgotten by
O be forgiven for salt bites I took.
Who drew me off last, willy-nilly, live
On (darling) free. If we meet, know me by
Your own exempt (I pray) and earthly look.

A 'broken heart' . . but *can* a heart break, now?
Lovers have stood bareheaded in love's 'storm'
Three thousand years, changed by their mistress' 'charm',
Fitted their 'torment' to a passive bow,
Suffered the 'darts' under a knitted brow,
And has one heart *broken* for all this 'harm'?
An arm is something definite. My arm
Is acting—I hardly know to tell you how.

It aches . . well, after fifteen minutes of
Serving, I can't serve more, it's not my arm,
A piece of pain joined to me, helpless dumb thing.
After four months of work-destroying love
(An hour, I still don't lift it: I feel real alarm:
Weeks of this,—no doctor finds a thing),
    not much; and not all. Still, this is something.

A spot of poontang on a five-foot piece,
Diminutive, but room *enough* . . like clay
To finger eager on some torrid day . .
Who'd throw her black hair back, and hang, and tease.
Never, not once in all one's horny lease
To have had a demi-lay, a pretty, gay,
Snug, slim and supple-breasted girl for play . .
She bats her big, warm eyes, and slides like grease.

And cuff her silly-hot again, mouth hot
And wet her small round writhing—but this screams
Suddenly awake, unreal as alkahest,
My God, this isn't what I *want!*—You tot
The harrow-days you hold me to, black dreams,
The dirty water to get off my chest.

Three, almost, now into the ass's years,
When hard on burden burden galls my back,
I carry corn feeds others, only crack
Cudgels, kicks on me, mountainous arrears
Worsen—avulse my fiery shirt!—The spheres
May sing with pain, I grieve knee-down, I slack
Deeper in evil . . love's demoniac
Jerguer, who frisked me, hops aside and jeers.

The dog's and monkey's years—pot's residue,
Growling and toothless, giggling, grimacing—
I hope to miss. Who in my child could see
The adulter and bizarre of thirty-two?—
But I will seem more silent soon . . mire-king.
Time, time that damns, disvexes. Unman me.

Began with swirling, blind, unstilled oh still,—
The tide had set in toward the western door
And I was working with the tide, I bore
My panful of reflexion firm, until
A voice arrested me,—body, and will,
And panful, wheeled and spilt, tempted nerves tore,
And all uncome time blackened like the core
Of an apple on through man's heart moving still . .

At nine o'clock and thirty Thursday night,
In Nineteen XXXX, February
Twice-ten-day, by a doorway in McIntosh,
So quietly neither the rip's cold slosh
Nor the meshing of great wheels warned me, unwary,
An enigmatic girl smiled out my sight.

Darling I wait O in my upstairs box
O for your footfall, O for your footfáll
in the extreme heat—I don't mind at all,
it's silence has me and the no of clocks
keeping us isolated longer: rocks
did the first martyr and will do to stall
our enemies, I'll get up on the roof of the hall
and heave freely. The University of Soft Knocks

will headlines in the *Times* make: Fellow goes mad,
crowd panics, rhododendrons injured. Slow
will flow the obituaries while the facts get straight,
almost straight. He was in love and he was had.
That was it: he should have stuck to his own mate,
before he went a-coming across the sea-O.

I owe you, do I not, a roofer: though
My sister-*in*-law and her nephews stayed,
Not I stayed. O kind sister-outlaw, laid
Far off and legally four weeks, stoop low,
For my true thanks are fugitive also
Only to you;—stop off your cant, you jade,
Bend down,—*I* have not ever disobeyed
You; and you will hear what it is I owe.

I owe you thanks for evenings in that house
When . . neither here, nor there, no where, were you,
Nights like long knives; . . *two* letters! . . times when your
    voice
Nearly I latched. Another debit to
Your kinder husband. From the country of Choice
Another province chopt,—and they were few.

Ménage à trois, like Tristan's,—difficult! . .
The convalescent Count; his mistress; fast
The wiry wild arthritic young fantast
In love with her, his genius occult,
His weakness blazing, ugly, an insult
A salutation; in his yacht they assed
Up and down the whole coast six months . . last
It couldn't: . . the pair to Paris. Chaos, result.

Well—but four worse!! . . all four, marvellous friends—
Some horse-shit here, eh?—You admitted it,
Come, you did once . . and we *are friends*, I say.—
'La Cuchiani aima Tristan, mais . .'
(The biographer says) *unscrupulous* a bit,
Or utterly . . . There, of course, the resemblance ends.

'Ring us up when you want to see us . .' —'Sure,'
Said Moses to the SS woman, smil-
ing hopeless Moses.—Put her whip and file
Away and walked away, strip-murderer,
A svelte Lise, whistling . . . Knowing, it's all *your*
(Alas) initiation: *you* I can't: while
We are relationless, 'us'?—Hail, chat: cant, heil!—
Hypocrite-perfect! hoping *I* endure.

A winter-shore is forming in my eye,
The widest river: down to it we dash,
In love, but I am naked, and shake; so,
Uncoloured-thick-oil clad, you nod and cry
 Let's go!' . . white fuzzless limbs you razor flash,
And I am to follow the way you go.

27 August

Christian to Try: "I am so coxed in it,
All I can do is pull, pull without shame,
Backwards,—on the coxswain fall the fiery blame,
I slump free and exhausted."—"Stop a bit,"
Try studied his sloe gin, "if you must fit
A trope so, you must hope to quit the game"
Pursued my brown friend with the plausible name
"Before your heart enlarging mucks you. Minute
By minute you pull faster."—But I too
Am named, though lost . . you learn God's will, give in,
After, whatever, you sit on, you sit.
Try "Quit" said "and be free." I freeze to you
And I am free now of the fire of this sin
I choose . . I lose, yes . . but then I submit!

I break my pace now for a sonic boom,
the future's with & in us. I sit fired
but comes on strong with the fire fatigue: I'm tired.
'I'd drive my car across the living-room
if I could get it inside the house.' You loom
less, less than before when your voice choired
into my transept hear I now it, not expired
but half-dead with exhaustion, like Mr Bloom.

Dazzle, before I abandon you, my eyes,
my eyes which I need for journeys difficult
in which case it may be said that I survive you.
Your voice continues, with its lows & highs,
and I am a willing accomplice in the cult
and every word that I   have gasped of you is true.

'I didn't see anyone else, I just saw Lise'
Anne Frank remorseful from the grave: ah well,
it was a vision of her mother in Hell,
a payment beforehand for rebellion's seize,
whereby she grew up: springing from her knees
she saw her parents level. I ward your spell
away, and I try hard to look at you level
but that is quite unaccustomed to me, Lise.

Months I lookt up, entranced by you up there
like a Goya ceiling which will not come down,
in swirling clouds, until the end is here.
Tetélestai. We steamed in a freighter from Spain
& I will never see those frescoes again
nor need to, having memorized your cloudy gown.

You come blonde visiting through the black air
knocking on my hinged lawn-level window
and you will come for years, above, below,
& through to interrupt my study where
I'm sweating it out like asterisks: so there,—
you are the text, my work's broken down so
I found, after my grandmother died, slow,
and I had flown far South to her funeral spare

but crowded with relations, I found her last
letter unopened, much less answered: shame
overcame me so far I paused & cried
in my underground study, for all the past
undone & never again to walk tall, lame
at the mercy of your presence to abide.

All we were going strong last night this time,
the *mots* were flying & the frozen daiquiris
were downing, supine on the floor lay Lise
listening to Schubert grievous & sublime,
my head was frantic with a following rime:
it was a good evening, an evening to please,
I kissed her in the kitchen—ecstasies—
among so much good we tamped down the crime.

The weather's changing. This morning was cold,
as I made for the grove, without expectation,
some hundred Sonnets in my pocket, old,
to read her if she came. Presently the sun
yellowed the pines & my lady came not
in blue jeans & a sweater. I sat down & wrote.